Digital Etherealism (*Luminum Sculptura*)

An Artistic Genre, Movement and Manifesto

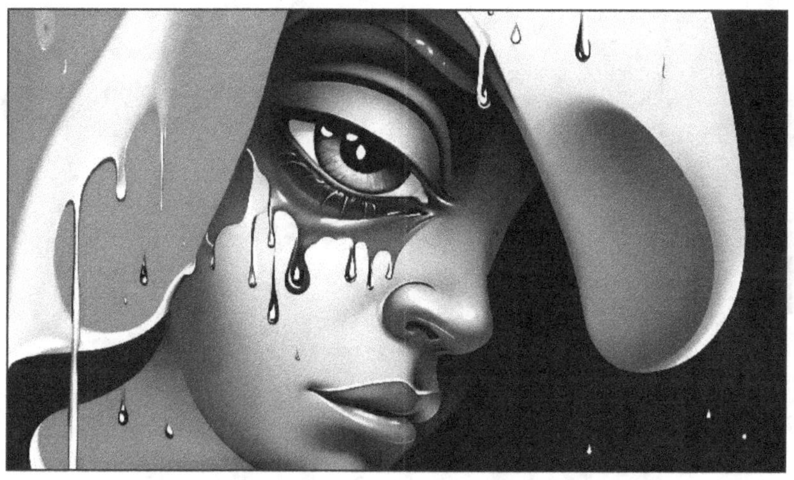

Giuseppe Antonio Ippolito Macaluso
Ph.D., MFA

Table of Contents

Prolouge: *Evolutionary Roots and Bridges*

Digital Etherealism emerges as the organic evolution of traditional photography, nurtured by the transformative capabilities of digital painting techniques. Rooted in the rich soil of photographic heritage, this movement germinates from the seeds of capturing reality through lenses. However, as technology advances, we transcend mere documentary or recorded imagery.

The alchemy begins with the infusion of digital tools, where the ephemera of light becomes brushes, and canvases expand into boundless digital landscapes. Employing techniques of *Luminum Sculptura* "light sculpting" through meticulous digital painting techniques, we breathe life into static photographs, transcending the confines of realism. The marriage of traditional and digital media births a new visual language – one that speaks to the soul, transcending the limitations of the physical mediums, and traditional formal pictorial expectations.

This movement is not confined to its origin; it acts as a catalyst for the evolution of other bridge media. Like a river flowing through diverse landscapes, **Digital Etherealism** carves pathways for the convergence of different, not only photographic, artistic disciplines. The alchemical process that reshapes traditional photography serves as a beacon, inviting artists from various realms to explore uncharted territories.

As a result, this movement acts as a nexus, connecting photography and digital art in a symbiotic dance. It beckons artists to bridge gaps, to traverse the realms between light and pigments, between the tangible and the ethereal. Through its evolution, **Digital Etherealism** becomes not only a movement but a fertile ground for the growth of other artistic expressions, fostering a diverse landscape where traditional and digital elements coalesce in unprecedented harmony.

A New Art Genre & Movement

Digital Etherealism is an innovative art genre and movement that seamlessly melds the ethereal qualities of traditional art with the transformative power of digital technologies.

Just as photography challenged the dominance of painting by capturing reality with unprecedented accuracy, **Digital Etherealism** emerges as a new paradigm, blurring the lines between artistic representation and the intangible realm of dreams, emotions, and surreal narratives through transformative digital techniques. This fusion of the ethereal and the digital echoes the historical shift from painting to photography, pushing the boundaries of artistic expression and inviting viewers to embark on a captivating journey into the sublime.

Artists within this genre utilize digital tools and techniques to create dreamlike, otherworldly compositions that transcend the boundaries of reality. The essence of **Digital Etherealism** lies in capturing and accentuating the intangible, such as emotions, atmospheres, and surreal narratives, through a harmonious blend of image capture and generation, digital painting, manipulation, and imaginative storytelling. The result is a body of work that invites viewers to experience a digital realm where the ethereal and the tangible coalesce, offering a unique and immersive journey into the sublime.

Manifesto: Digital Etherealism

Manifesto of Digital Etherealism (*Luminum Sculptura*)

I. Preamble

In the crucible where technology fuses with artistic expression, we herald the dawn of **Digital Etherealism** – an avant-garde movement surging beyond the bounds of perception and reality. As stewards of this era, we unite to breathe life into a vision that seamlessly merges the ethereal with the digital, forging a new frontier in artistic exploration.

We reside in an era of profound transformation, where technology evolves at an unprecedented pace, reshaping our understanding of the world. The dichotomy between the tangible and the virtual dissolves, and a realm of new artistic possibilities unfolds.

Digital Etherealism emerges as a testament to embracing change. We believe in harnessing technology to craft art that is visually captivating and imbued with profound meaning. Our mission is to push the boundaries of creativity, dismantling traditional barriers and birthing a novel form of artistic expression.

We are a collective of diverse artists, creators from every corner of the globe, joining forces to articulate our vision of a revolutionary art movement.

Digital Etherealism is not merely an artistic revolution; it is a cultural metamorphosis.

II. Essence

Digital Etherealism is grounded in the conviction that the ephemeral and the technological can exist in perfect harmony. Our art unravels the intangible facets of the human experience – rendering emotions, atmospheres, and imaginative narratives with a transcendent touch. The digital realm becomes a powerful tool for expressing the ephemeral, offering new ways to experience and understand the world around us.

Our inspiration spans the breadth of nature, music, literature, and philosophy. Drawn to the enigma of the natural world, we believe the digital realm can evoke wonder and awe. Our art serves to explore complex ideas and emotions in innovative ways.

Using various digital tools, including digital imaging and painting, we are perpetual experimenters. We believe the potential of digital art is limitless, and our creations aim to be visually intriguing and thought-provoking, inviting viewers into a world where the ethereal and the tangible converge.

III. Mediums

The digital canvas is our primary medium, a realm where creation transcends traditional boundaries. Through a symphony of digital painting, alteration, and groundbreaking storytelling, we craft compositions existing in the liminal spaces between dreams and reality.

Our work is not a mere collection of pixels or lines of code; it is a living, breathing world that beckons the viewer to step inside and explore. Immersive experiences are our hallmark, transporting the viewer to uncharted realms through our mastery of digital tools.

Whether it be a surreal landscape, an avant-garde vision, or a character from a beloved story, our work embodies a unique style and vision. We continually push the limits of what is achievable with digital art.

IV. Transformation

Digital Etherealism champions the transformative power of art. We believe art can change lives, challenge beliefs, and broaden minds to new possibilities. Each stroke, pixel, mote, and narrative thread is a vessel for metamorphosis, inviting viewers to witness the evolution of the tangible into the sublime.

Art is a formidable instrument for change, and we are devoted to using it to create a more visually rich and just world.

V. Narrative Alchemy

Our creations are not mere documentary images; they are stories waiting to unravel. Through narrative alchemy, we infuse our works with depth, inviting spectators into immersive worlds that provoke thought, stir emotions, and transport minds beyond the constraints of the mundane.

Every image holds the potential to be a vessel for storytelling. By meticulously crafting composition, lighting, and color palette, we create visual narratives that are visually intriguing and thought-provoking.

Our objective is to create images that linger in the minds of viewers, extending beyond mere aesthetics to become catalysts for thought and inspiration.

VI. Synergistic Aesthetics

We honor the marriage of traditional craftsmanship and the evolution brought forth by the digital realm, cherishing the fusion of the old and the new. We embrace the dynamic interplay of chaos and order, unearthing a beauty that surpasses conventional art.

Art's beauty lies in its ability to transcend time and place. Traditional craftsmanship, a time-honored art form reflecting history and culture, converges with digital art, a dynamic form shaped by evolving technologies. This synergistic aesthetic mirrors the ever-changing world we inhabit – a beauty both timeless and contemporary.

VII. Embracing Connectivity

In the realm of **Digital Etherealism**, we wholeheartedly acknowledge the profound interconnectedness among all things. Through this deep understanding, we cultivate a vibrant community of like-minded artists, collaborators, and enthusiasts, united by a common drive to push the boundaries of artistry.

Within our community, we nurture an environment of mutual support and open dialogue, recognizing that our collective voice gains potency through these relationships. By sharing knowledge, experiences, and creative endeavors, we amplify the resonance of our combined artistry, sparking inspiration and innovation.

Through genuine connection and collaboration, we pave the way for endless possibilities and groundbreaking artistic achievements that can shape our world and leave an enduring mark on the artistic landscape.

VIII. Advocacy

As advocates of **Digital Etherealism**, we champion the democratization of artistic expression. We encourage experimentation, exploration, and the dismantling of traditional barriers hindering artists from fully expressing themselves. In doing so, we empower artists to embrace the limitless possibilities offered by the intersection of the ethereal and the digital.

Digital Etherealism is a potent tool capable of creating innovative forms of art. We urge artists to wield this tool to explore their creativity and push the boundaries of what is possible. **Digital Etherealism** possesses the potential to positively transform the world, and we are committed to assisting artists in using these tools to make a lasting impact.

IX. Legacy

We envisage a legacy where **Digital Etherealism** stands as a cornerstone in the evolution of art. As we navigate uncharted creative territories, we leave behind a trail of inspiration, challenging future generations to embark on their own odyssey of artistic exploration.

Digital Etherealism possesses the potential to revolutionize how we create and experience art. By combining the best of traditional art with cutting-edge technology, we can forge new forms of expression that are both visually intriguing and profoundly meaningful.

X. Unveiling the Unseen

In **Digital Etherealism**, we are the alchemists of the unseen. Through our creations, we invite the world to witness the unveiling of the ethereal – a testament to the boundless potential of the human imagination and the transformative power of art in the digital age.

The ethereal exists beyond the physical realm, in the realm of spirit and possibility. It is the realm of dreams, imagination, and inspiration – a realm where anything is possible.

In **Digital Etherealism**, we seek to bring the ethereal into the physical world through our art. Using digital technology, we create images and experiences that capture the beauty and mystery of the unseen. Our works inspire, challenge, and transport viewers to a higher plane of existence. **Digital Etherealism** can open minds, break down barriers, and bring people together.

We are the vanguard of a movement that transcends the ordinary, unveiling the unseen for the world to behold. Welcome to Digital Etherealism – where the ethereal and the digital converge in a symphony of artistic expression.

Comparing Digital Etherealism to other artistic genres and manifestos:

Similarities:

Surrealism: Both explore the realm of dreams, emotions, and the subconscious, creating fantastical and dreamlike imagery that transcends reality. Both utilize innovative techniques and challenge traditional artistic boundaries.

Compare: Surrealists often relied on automatism and unexpected juxtapositions, while **Digital Etherealism** emphasizes digital tools and manipulation.

Romanticism: Both place focus on nature, emotional expression, and the sublime. Both seek to evoke awe and wonder in the viewer.

Compare: Romantics relied on landscape paintings and dramatic imagery, while **Digital Etherealism** utilizes digital spaces and spatially unbounded atmospheres.

Abstract Expressionism: Both prioritize emotional expression and the power of the subconscious over representational accuracy. Both emphasize the artist's subjective experience and use innovative techniques to push artistic boundaries.

Compare: Abstract Expressionists used gestural painting and spontaneity, while **Digital Etherealism** uses digital tools and manipulation to achieve similar effects.

Differences:

Medium: **Digital Etherealism** is unique in its focus on the digital medium, utilizing specific tools and techniques like "*Luminum Sculptura*" to achieve its effects. Other genres generally focus on traditional mediums like painting, sculpture, or film.

Technological Influence: **Digital Etherealism** is a direct product of advances in technology, shaping its aesthetic and capabilities. Many other genres may incorporate technology but are not inherently defined by it, with the exception of photography.

Accessibility: The manifesto emphasizes democratization and the accessibility of **Digital Etherealism**. This sets it apart from previous movements that might have been dominated by elite artists or specific schools of thought.

Comparison of Manifestos:

Futurism: Both manifestos are characterized by boldness, a desire to break with the past, and a belief in the transformative power of new technologies.

Differences: Futurism focused on celebrating urbanism, speed, and technology as inherently modern, while **Digital Etherealism** prioritizes the ethereal and intangible, seeking an evolutionary balance between traditional and digital.

Surrealist Manifesto: Both aim to explore the unconscious mind and challenge conventional perceptions.

Differences: The Surrealist Manifesto emphasizes automatic writing and dream analysis, while **Digital Etherealism** emphasizes digital tools and manipulation, creating a more visually-oriented experience.

Afterword

To clarify an important point, the described phenomenon, "**Digital Etherealism** (*Luminum Sculptura*)," encapsulates characteristics of both an *art genre* and an *art movement*.

Art Genre:
An art genre typically refers to a specific style, technique, or approach within the broader realm of artistic expression.

Digital Etherealism is considered an art genre because it defines a distinctive style of art-making that involves the fusion of traditional and digital mediums, emphasizing techniques such as "*Luminum Sculptura*" (light sculpting) and digital painting.

Digital Etherealism intentionally *avoids confining artists to prescribed technical or visual rules*. The genre is characterized by its emphasis on crafting imagery that deliberately goes beyond traditional artistic boundaries, fostering a creative environment that encourages dreamlike applications of techniques and compositions. This intentional departure from conventional norms distinguishes **Digital Etherealism** as a distinct and defined genre within the expansive landscape of digital art.

Art Movement:
An art movement usually encompasses a broader cultural, philosophical, or ideological shift within the art world. Movements often involve a collective of artists sharing common goals, principles, and a reaction to the existing artistic norms.

Digital Etherealism is also an art movement due to its emphasis on embracing technological advancements, pushing the boundaries of traditional art forms, and fostering a community of like-minded artists united by a shared vision.

Digital Etherealism emphasizes principles, such as the transformative power of art, advocacy for democratization, and the creation of a legacy, thus aligning it with the characteristics of an art movement.

In conclusion, **Digital Etherealism** (*Luminum Sculptura*) can be described as both an art genre and an art movement. It defines a specific style and technique (genre) while also embodying a collective and transformative spirit that aligns with the broader concept of an art movement.

Bibliographic References: General references on Digital Etherealism

Evolution and Bridges:

Ippolito, J.A. (2023). *AI Collaboration: The Future of Creativity and Productivity: A Guide for Everyone*. Golden Quill Veritas. (Explores the utilization of artificial intelligence technologies as collaborative partners in creativity.)

Galloway, A. R. (2012). *Interface Culture: How New Technologies Are Transforming the Way We Create and Communicate*. Routledge. (Explores the relationship between technology and artistic expression, particularly relevant to the text's emphasis on digital tools and the evolution of photography.)

Crary, J. (2001). Images Are Not Things: Essays on Seeing. MIT Press. * (Examines the relationship between images and their physical realities, aligning with the text's discussion of transcending the limitations of photography.)

Hansen, M. B. N. (2000). *Embodied Sensorium: Technologies of Bodily Knowing*. Stanford University Press. (Analyzes the ways in which technology shapes our perception and experience, relevant to the text's idea of

"*Luminum Sculptura*" shaping how we engage with images.)

Aesthetic and Technique:

Wildermuth, S., & Rosen, M. (2015). *Beyond the Canvas: The Digital Transformation of Painting*. Bloomsbury Publishing. (Explores the impact of digital technologies on painting practices, providing context for the text's discussion of digital painting techniques.)

Lury, J. (2013). *Atmospheric Images: Cinematic Phenomenology and Virtual Worlds*. University of Minnesota Press. (Analyzes the role of atmosphere and mood in visual culture, valuable for understanding the text's focus on emotional atmospheres and ethereal qualities.)

Fried, M. (2008). *Absorption and Theatricality: Pagan Theories of Painting*. Princeton University Press. (Discusses the tension between immersion and the awareness of artifice in art, relevant to the text's blending of the tangible and the ethereal.)

Impact and Legacy:

Bolter, J. D., & Gruenberg, R. (2009). *Remediation: The Logic of Media*. MIT Press. (Explores the ways in which new media forms adapt and reinterpret characteristics of earlier ones, useful for understanding the text's view of **Digital Etherealism** as both rooted in photography and surpassing it.)

Bown, P. (2012). *How Algorithms Shape Our World*. University of Chicago Press. (Examines the role of algorithms and technology in shaping culture and artistic expression, relevant to the text's call for democratizing artistic creation through digital tools.)

Bostrom, N. (2003). *Are We Living in a Computer Simulation?*. Oxford University Press. (Investigates the potential impact of advanced technology on our understanding of reality and perception, aligning with the text's interest in exploring the "unseen" and the boundaries of perception.)

Dyer, S., & Green, P. H. (Eds.). (2007). *Digital Art: A Critical Introduction*. Thames & Hudson.

Graham, S. B. (2018). *Digital Dreams: How New Technologies Are Transforming the Way We Think and Feel*. Penguin Books.

Mitchell, W. J. T. (2005). *What Do Pictures Want? The New History of Visual Representation*. University of Chicago Press.

Surrealism:

Breton, A. (1972). *Manifestoes of Surrealism* (R. Seaver, Trans.). Harper & Row.

Ruby, P. (2008). *Surrealism and Art*. Phaidon Press.

Shrigley, E. W. (2006). *Salvador Dalí*. Taschen.

Romanticism:

Abrams, M. H. (1971). *Natural Supernaturalism: Tradition and Revolution in Romantic Literature*. W.W. Norton & Company.

Gilman, E. B. (1970). *The Romantic Movement in English Literature*. Oxford University Press.

Wolf, L. (2007). *Romanticism: Literature and Science on the Edge of the Known*. Cornell University Press.

Abstract Expressionism:

Fried, M. (1998). *Greenberg and American Art.* University of Chicago Press.

Hobsbawm, E. (1994). *Age of Extremes: The Short Twentieth Century, 1914-1991*. Abacus.

Rosenthal, R. (1960). *Jackson Pollock.* Abrams.

Futurism:

Marinetti, F. T. (2009). *Manifesto of Futurism*. Penguin Books.

Spinetti, T. (1977). *Futurism: An Anthology*. Yale University Press.

Tisdale, D. (1970). *Futurist Manifesto*. Vintage Books.